A KID'S GUIDE TO DIY

A BOOK OF TRICKS AND PRACTICAL JOKES

for Kids Who Love to Prank

Rotting eggs

Jell-O-Worm sandwich

Bigfoot was here!

by Ruth Owen

WINDMILL BOOKS

Published in 2022 by Windmill Books,
an Imprint of Rosen Publishing
29 East 21st Street, New York, NY 10010

Produced for Rosen by Ruth Owen Books
Designer: Emma Randall
Photos courtesy of Ruth Owen Books and Shutterstock

Photo Credits:
Cover, 1, 3, 5, 6-7, 8-9, 10-11, 13, 14-15, 16, 20-21 © Shutterstock; Cover, 1, 4-5, 6-7, 8-9, 10-11, 12, 14-15, 16-17, 18-19, 22-23, 24-25, 26-27, 28-29 © Ruby Tuesday Books and John Such.

Cataloging-in-Publication Data

Names: Owen, Ruth.
Title: A book of tricks and practical jokes for kids who love to prank / Ruth Owen.
Description: New York : Windmill Books, 2022. | Series: A kid's guide to DIY | Includes glossary and index.
Identifiers: ISBN 9781538270417 (pbk.) | ISBN 9781538270431 (library bound) | ISBN 9781538270424 (6 pack) | ISBN 9781538270448 (ebook)
Subjects: LCSH: Practical jokes--Juvenile literature. | Tricks--Juvenile literature.
Classification: LCC PN6231.P67 O94 2022 | DDC 818'.5402--dc23

Manufactured in the United States of America

CPSIA Compliance Information: Batch BSWM22: For Further Information contact Rosen Publishing, New York, New York at 1-800-237-9932

CONTENTS

WARNING

Neither the author nor the publisher shall be liable for any bodily harm or damage to property that may happen as a result of carrying out the practical jokes in this book.

ARE YOU A PRANKSTER?

Want to horrify your friends by getting them to bite into worm sandwiches? Or how about faking a terrible tear in the wallpaper and freaking out your mom? If these pranks sound like fun, then this book of **practical jokes** is for you!

A practical joke is usually played on one or more people, and the idea behind it is to confuse, embarrass, or surprise the **victim**. Victims of a practical joke are always let in on the joke in the end, however, and get to laugh at themselves along with the joker who played the trick.

These types of jokes are called "practical" because unlike a **verbal joke**, they involve equipment or **props** and need to be planned and set up in advance.

In this book, you will be getting practical creating props such as giant cardboard feet and green fried eggs. So get planning and making, and pull some cool, not-too-cruel practical jokes on your friends and family!

A WORM SNACK

Just picture the scene: your friend is hungry. You make them a delicious sandwich. And then, just before they take a big bite, you shout, "What's that wriggling in your sandwich?" The fantastic worm sandwich prank is guaranteed to create screams of horror. But thankfully, the worms are only made of Jell-O and are not real.

Worms are fascinating creatures that help make soil healthy. They eat dead plants and animals and then excrete out **nutrients** that living plants need as food.

All that wormy science stuff is cool. But what's also cool about worms is that they have the power to totally gross people out. And where there's the power to gross out, there's **potential** for a practical joke!

GOTCHA!

YOU WILL NEED:

- 100 flexible straws
- A tall container such as a juice carton
- A rubber band
- 10 ounces (280 g) of raspberry Jell-O
- 0.4 ounce (12 g) unflavored powdered gelatin
- A mixing bowl and spoon
- 2 pints (950 ml) boiling water
- 1 cup of whipping cream
- Green food coloring
- Bread and lettuce

STEP 1: You will be using the straws as a mold to make the Jell-O worms, so begin by pulling out, or flexing, the straws to make the ridged part as long as possible.

STEP 2: Place the straws into the container. You will need a tight fit to keep the straws upright. You can use a rubber band to keep them tightly together in a bundle.

STEP 3: Place the Jell-O and unflavored gelatin in a bowl. Then add the boiling water and allow the Jell-O and gelatin to dissolve in the water.

STEP 4: When the mixture is just warm, begin adding small quantities of the cream and just a few drops of green food coloring at a time. Stir thoroughly. Keep adding cream and food coloring until your worm mixture is the color you want it to be.

STEP 5: Slowly pour the mixture into the straws. It's no problem if some mixture leaks out of the bottom of the straws into the container. Just keep filling the straws until the container is filled or all the mixture is gone.

A tall glass also makes a good container for the straws.

STEP 6: Leave the Jell-O worms to set in a refrigerator overnight.

STEP 7: When the worm mixture is set firm, carefully remove the bundle of straws from the container and separate them.

STEP 8: Starting at one end of a straw, use your fingers to gently squeeze the Jell-O worm from the straw.

STEP 9: When your Jell-O worms are ready, make a worm and lettuce sandwich and get ready to gross out your friends!

THE PULLED THREAD

Got someone in your life who makes it their business to keep trying to neaten you up? Then this trick is guaranteed to drive them crazy! And what's more, it's super quick and easy to set up.

STEP 1:

Thread the needle.

STEP 2:

Push the needle through the front of the shirt and pull the thread out through the neck hole. Leave about 1 inch (2.5 cm) of thread hanging on the front of the shirt.

STEP 3: Take the needle off the thread. Carefully put on the shirt and then tuck the long piece of thread inside the shirt.

YOU WILL NEED:

- A plain colored shirt or T-shirt
- A needle
- A long piece of white thread

STEP 4: When people spot a small loose thread on your shirt, they won't be able to resist trying to remove it. As the thread is pulled, however, instead of coming away from the shirt, it will get longer and longer and longer.

BAZINGA!

THAT'S TORN IT!

There's a terrible tear in the wallpaper! The adults are furious! So why are you struggling to contain your laughter as you get scolded? Because you know you've just pulled the classic torn wallpaper prank—and what's more, everyone's fallen for it!

STEP 1: Fold the piece of paper in half.

STEP 2: Starting where the paper is creased, tear a diamond shape from the paper.

STEP 3: Open up the diamond, turn it over, and attach small blobs of putty to the top half.

YOU WILL NEED:

- A room that has wallpaper
- A small piece of white paper
- Some sticky poster putty

STEP 4: Now press the top half of the diamond onto a wall where there is wallpaper. Allow the bottom half to hang loose. The white paper will look just like a tear in the wallpaper.

STEP 5: When the "tear" is discovered, take the blame, or deny all knowledge. See how long you can go without laughing!

ROTTING EGGS TRICK

You might think you'd need to use paint to turn eggs green and make them look as if they are rotting. But amazingly this can be done with a red cabbage. So how does it work?

The colors in vegetables are made by materials called **pigments**. When the purplish-red pigment of red cabbage mixes with egg white, however, a chemical reaction takes place that turns the egg white green.

Cook a green egg and serve it to a friend. Or you can serve your friend a normal egg and give yourself a green egg. Then, as he or she watches in horror as you dig into your egg, say, "Oh, it's just a little moldy. I'm sure it will be fine!"

YOU WILL NEED:

- Red cabbage
- A knife and cutting board
- A saucepan
- Water
- Eggs
- Two small bowls (for separating the egg yolk from the egg white)
- A dessert spoon
- Cooking oil or butter
- A frying pan
- A spatula or egg turner
- A plate for serving

STEP 1: Chop up half a cup of red cabbage.

STEP 2: Place the cabbage in the saucepan with two cups of water. Bring the water to a boil on the stove, then turn down the heat and cook the cabbage on low heat for about 10 minutes. The water will turn purplish-red with juices from the cabbage.

STEP 3: Allow the colored water to cool. You can keep it in the refrigerator for up to a week.

STEP 4: Crack an egg by tapping it on the edge of a bowl. Separate the egg yolk from the white by gently prying apart the two halves of the shell and allowing the white to run from the shell into a bowl.

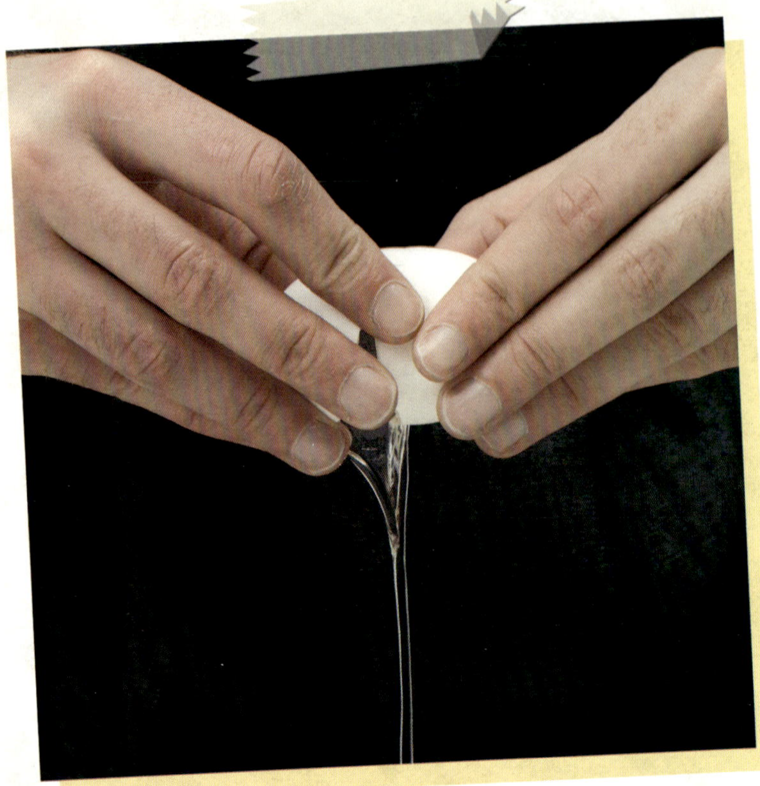

STEP 5: Mix one dessert spoonful of cabbage water into the egg white. The egg white will immediately turn green!

STEP 6: To cook the egg, put a little oil or butter in the frying pan and put the pan onto the stove. Pour the egg white into the pan and start frying.

STEP 7: Now pour the egg yolk onto the green egg white in the frying pan. Be very gentle so the yolk doesn't break. Fry the egg until fully cooked.

The green fried egg will look gruesome, but it is perfectly safe to eat and will taste just like a normal egg!

SODA ERUPTION

If you've ever put Mentos into a bottle of soda, you'll know it creates a frothy eruption of fizz! In this next practical joke, you'll learn how to set up a soda bottle so it will explode all over your victim, but they won't be able to tell that the soda tsunami is coming. Only carry out this prank if you're sure that no clothes, furniture, carpet, or other objects will be damaged.

STEP 1: Thread the needle. Push the needle through a mint and pull the thread through.

STEP 2: Tie a large knot in the end of the thread and then pull the thread through the mint up to the knot. Trim off any excess thread behind the knot.

YOU WILL NEED:

- A bottle of soda
- Mentos mints
- Thread and a large needle

STEP 3: Open the cap of the soda and carefully dangle the mint in the neck of the bottle. Screw the cap back on so it tightens over the thread and holds the mint in place.

STEP 4: Finally, cut the thread as close to the bottle cap as possible.

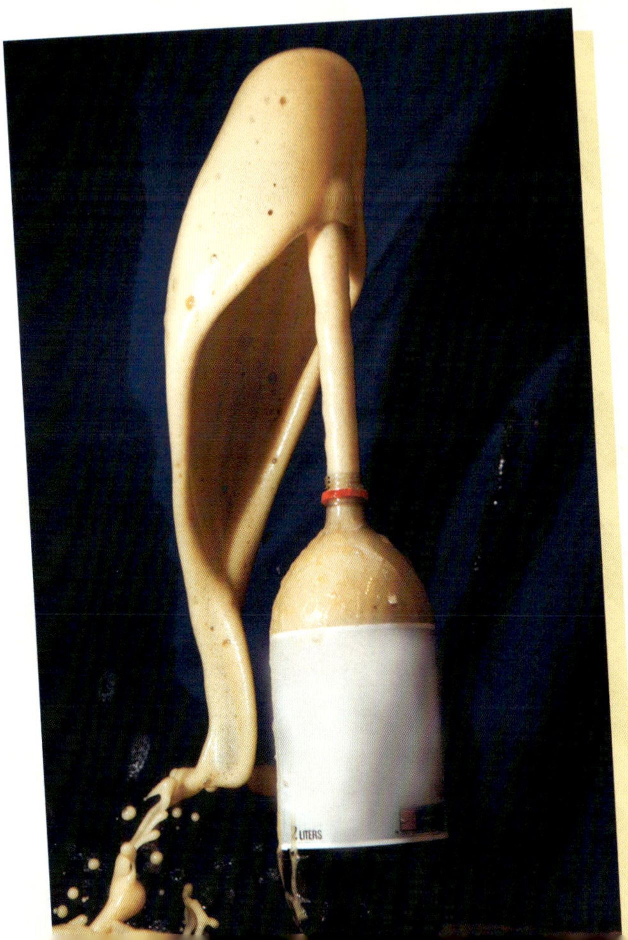

STEP 5: When your friend unscrews the bottle cap, the mint will drop into the soda and begin fizzing. Within seconds, the soda will explode!

Try threading two or three mints together for a more powerful effect. Your friend probably won't notice the mints in the neck of the bottle because he or she won't be looking for them or expecting them to be there.

SQUIRTING WATER BOTTLE

Got an empty water bottle in your family's recycling? It can be used to set up a fun prank to surprise and soak a friend. Make sure you recycle the bottle again once you've played the joke.

STEP 1: Fill the bottle with water so it is full to the very top. Screw on the cap tightly.

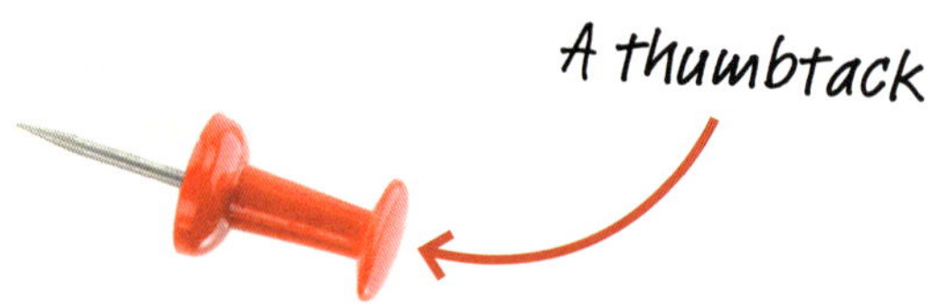

STEP 2: Pierce several holes around the base of the bottle using a thumbtack. A little water will squirt from each hole as you pierce it, but then the water will stop flowing.

As long as the bottle's cap stays screwed shut, the water won't squirt out of the holes.

Make the holes here.

YOU WILL NEED:

- A plastic bottle (choose a bottle made of hard, thick plastic)
- Water
- A thumbtack

STEP 3: Offer the bottle to a friend to drink from. As soon as he or she starts to unscrew the bottle's top, water will squirt from all the holes!

EXPLODING ENVELOPE

Want to play a practical joke that goes off with a bang? This exploding envelope prank takes a bit of preparation, but the **recipient** will be super shocked and surprised when their mail goes KABOOM!

The bang will be made by the "banger" from a party popper. Be ready, though, for a very loud noise. When the banger is no longer surrounded by the contents of the party popper, the noise it makes is much louder than usual.

STEP 1: Place the envelope face down. Using a craft knife, carefully unstick the envelope's right-hand edge and bottom edge.

Once the two edges are unstuck, open out the envelope.

YOU WILL NEED:

- A large envelope
- A craft knife
- A party popper
- Scissors
- Two pieces of cardboard
- A stapler
- A hot glue gun
- A glue stick

WARNING

Don't try out this joke on anyone who is easily scared or startled! Only use a glue gun if an adult is there to help you.

STEP 2: Cut open a party popper and remove the banger.

STEP 3: Cut the cardboard into two pieces. Each piece should be about half an inch (1 cm) narrower all the way around than the size of the envelope.

There should also be about a half-inch (1 cm) gap between the pieces of cardboard.

STEP 4: Now attach the party popper banger to the two pieces of cardboard. It must be firmly fixed in place so that the string absolutely cannot move.

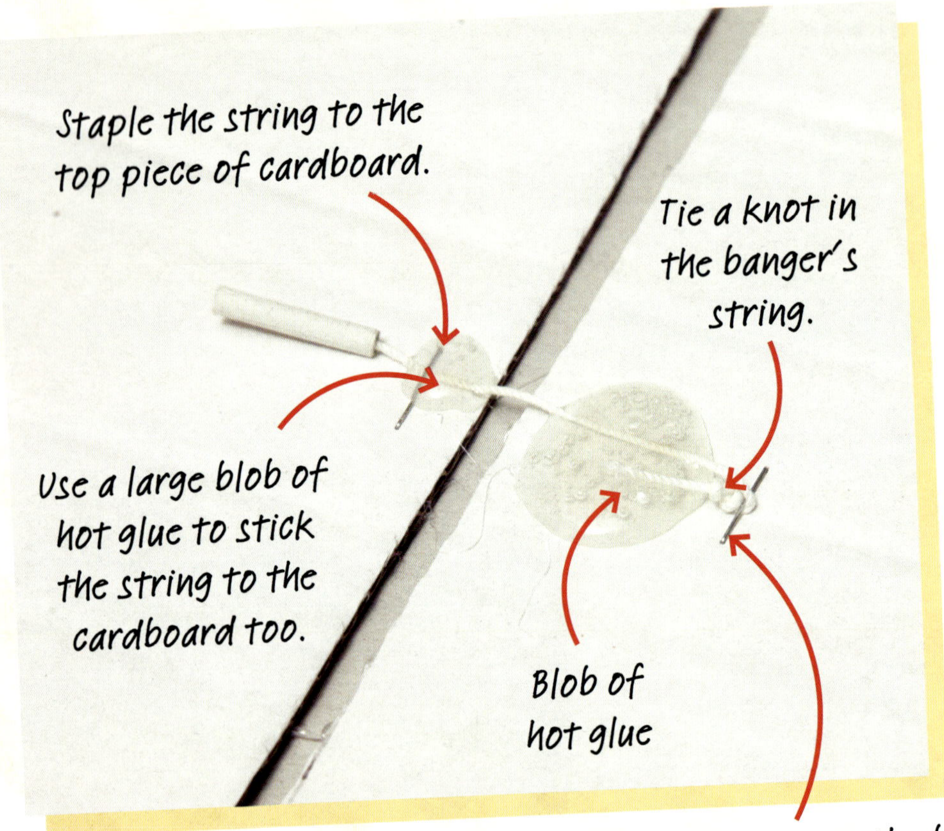

STEP 5: Glue the bottom piece of cardboard to the envelope.

STEP 6: Using a glue stick, reseal the bottom and right-hand edges of the envelope.

STEP 7: Address the envelope to your victim, and hand the envelope to him or her. The victim of the joke will take hold of the top piece of cardboard and pull it from the envelope.

As the cardboard is pulled, the banger's string (which is held in place by staples and glue) will tighten and then pull from the banger, setting off the banger's loud noise!

A BIGFOOT FOOTPRINT

Do you believe that Bigfoot exists? Many people do. Some even say that they've caught a glimpse of these giant half-ape, half-human beasts in forests and other wild places!

Eyewitnesses have reported sightings of Bigfeet that are 10 feet (3 m) tall. Footprints have even been found that are up to 27 inches (68.5 cm) long! Now, you can convince your neighbors that a Bigfoot is in town by creating fake **evidence** of a Bigfoot visit to your neighborhood. Build your own Bigfoot big feet, then make giant footprints in snow, soft mud, or sand where you can be sure a family member or neighbor will see them.

YOU WILL NEED:

- A large sheet of paper
- A pen
- Scissors
- Thick cardboard
- A craft knife
- A plank of wood and an adult to cut it into pieces
- A glue gun
- A pair of old sneakers
- Duct tape

STEP 1: Draw a template for your giant feet on the sheet of paper. Your big foot should be much bigger than a human foot. Cut out the paper template.

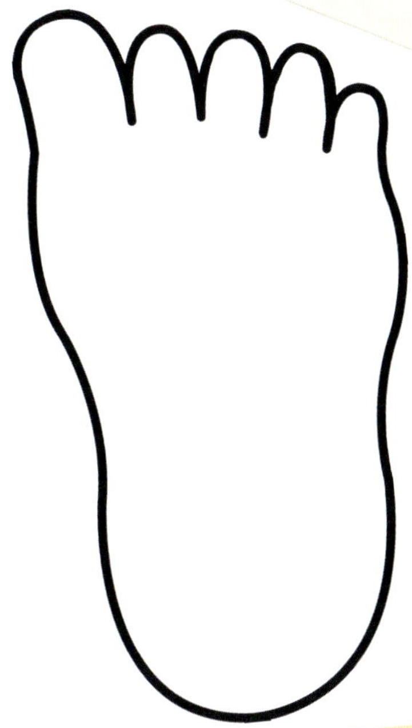

You only need to make one template because you can reverse it to make the second foot.

STEP 2: Lay the paper template onto the cardboard and draw around it. Cut out the cardboard foot shape using the craft knife.

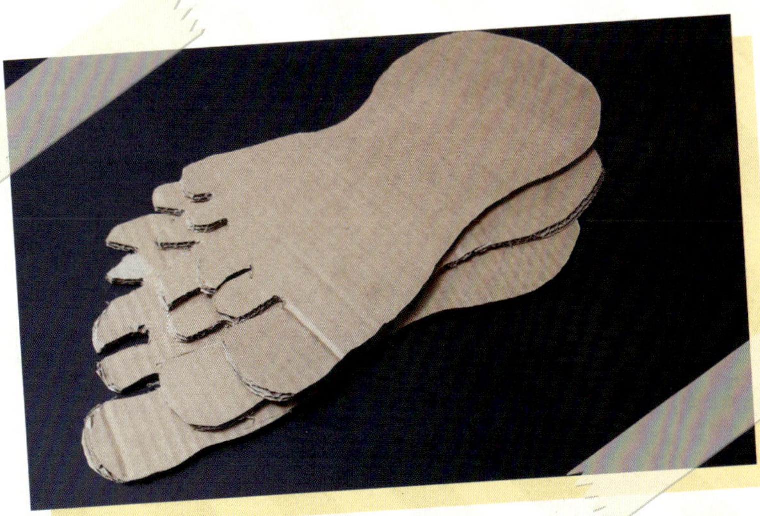

STEP 3: Repeat step 2 until you have three cardboard right feet and three left feet.

STEP 4: Ask an adult to cut two pieces of wood that are slightly longer than your cardboard feet.

STEP 5: Now put on the sneakers. While wearing the sneakers, tape them to the top side of each piece of wood using the duct tape.

Then wriggle your feet back out of the sneakers.

STEP 6: Now tape a cardboard foot to the underside of each piece of wood.

This is the underside of a completed foot.

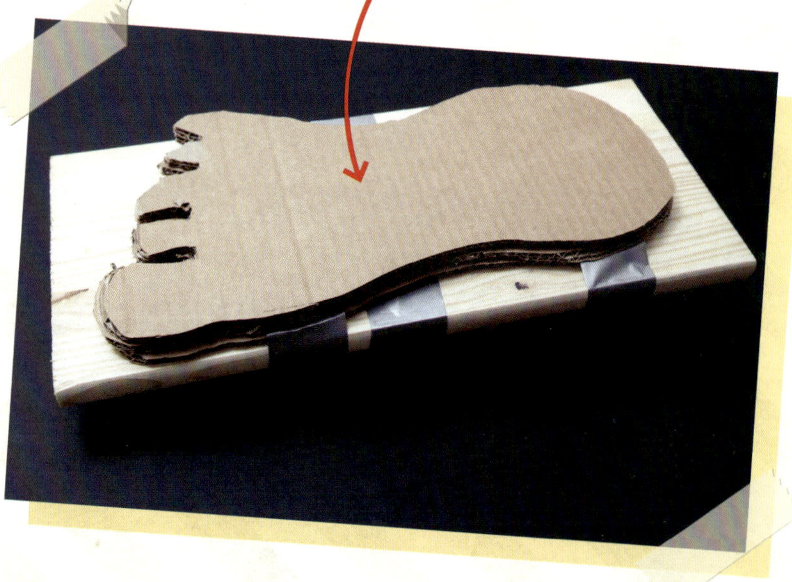

STEP 7: Now glue the second and third cardboard foot shape to the underside of each piece of wood. The three layers of cardboard will make a deep impression in snow, soft mud, or sand.

The top side of the completed feet.

STEP 8: Now put on your Bigfoot big feet and get busy making footprints.

When you've made some footprints, hide nearby to see people's reactions. Make sure you take photos of the Bigfoot prints as evidence of the creature's visit to your neighborhood!

Add an everyday item to your photo to show the size of the footprint.

GLOSSARY

evidence
Something that can prove or disprove a fact. For example, a footprint proves that a person or animal was in a particular place.

eyewitnesses
People who have personally seen something and are able to give a firsthand description of it.

nutrients
Substances that living things need to grow, get energy, and stay healthy. For example, vitamins and protein are nutrients.

pigments
Substances that give other materials their colors.

potential
The qualities or abilities that may be developed into something useful or successful in the future.

practical jokes
Jokes that involve practical work, such as making props, that are played on a victim to confuse, surprise, or embarrass that person.

props
Objects that are used in practical jokes, plays, movies, and TV shows. A prop might be a real object or a fake version, such as a fake bottle that is made from a material that looks like glass, but won't cut a person when it shatters.

recipient
A person who receives something, such as a piece of mail.

verbal joke
A joke that is told, or spoken.

victim
The person to whom something happens.

READ MORE

Fairclough, Wade David. *Pranklab: Practical Science Pranks You and Your Victim Can Learn From*. Naperville, IL: Sourcebooks Explore, 2021.

Shofner, Melissa Rae. *The Story Behind April Fools' Day*. New York: PowerKids Press, 2020.

Winterbottom, Julie. *Pranklopedia: The Funniest, Grossest, Craziest, Not-Mean Pranks on the Planet*. New York: Workman Publishing, 2016.

WEBSITES

https://www.fun-stuff-to-do.com/good-pranks.html

https://www.buzzfeed.com/mikespohr/17-easy-and-harmless-april-fools-pranks-for-kids

https://magictricksforkids.org/

Publisher's note to parents and teachers: Our editors have reviewed the websites listed here to make sure they're suitable for students. However, websites may change frequently. Please note that students should always be supervised when they access the internet.

INDEX